"He shall call upon Me, and I will answer him; I will be with him in trouble; I will deliver him and honor him"

Psalm 91:15 (NKJV)

Contributors

Pastor Rick Dressler
Trevor Burton
Just a Farmer
Pastor Dan Christiaan
Jeyran Main
Ethan Davenport
Pastor Andrew McCombe

LIVING IN LIGHT OF THE CROSS
MAGAZINE

COPYRIGHT © 2026
Living in Light of the Cross Magazine
This magazine may not be reproduced, either in part or in its entirety, in any form, by any means, without written permission from the publisher, with the exception of brief excerpts for purposes of radio, television, or published reviews. Although all possible means have been taken to ensure the accuracy of the material presented, Maple City Baptist Church is not liable for any misinterpretation, misapplication or typographical errors.
All rights, including the right of translation, are reserved.
Editor in Chief: S. Jeyran Main
Publisher: Review Tales Publishing & Editing Services
Cover Design: Samantha Egan
Designs: Pexels
ISBN 978-1-0699188-2-6 Paperback
ISBN 978-1-0699188-3-3 Digital
www.MapleCityBaptistChurch.com
For all inquiries please contact us directly.

Photo Credits from Pexels:
bertelli fotografia
brett jordan
davidex pedition
jibaro foto
nappy
pixa bay
rdne
tara winstead
tima miroshnichenko
yavuz eren gungor

Editor's Note

Dear Brothers and Sisters in Christ,

It is with great joy that I welcome you to this issue of the Maple City Church Magazine. Our theme for this season is one that reaches deep into the heart of every believer: the Psalms and the gift of prayer. As we journey together through these pages, my hope is that you are reminded of the beauty, honesty, and power found in speaking with God.

The book of Psalms is rich with songs, cries, praises, and confessions from people who walked through every imaginable circumstance. Their prayers—sometimes filled with confidence, sometimes with questions—show us that God invites us to come to Him just as we are. Whether we face uncertainty, joy, loss, or victory, the Psalms reassure us that our Heavenly Father listens. He is near. He is faithful.

Prayer is more than words we speak; it is the lifeline that connects us to God's heart. It anchors us when life feels unstable and lifts us when we feel weary. Through the Psalms, we learn that every moment of our lives can become a place of prayer—moments of praise, moments of lament, moments of quiet trust. As you read the reflections, testimonies, and teachings in this issue, may you be encouraged to draw closer to God, to speak with Him regularly, and to listen for His gentle leading.

It is my prayer that this magazine strengthens your faith, deepens your understanding of prayer, and guides you back into the comforting, powerful, timeless words of the Psalms. May every page bring you one step nearer to the God who loves you, hears you, and walks beside you in every season.

Jeyran Main

Editor,
Living in Light of the Cross

Praying like Paul

PASTOR RICK DRESSLER

The great apostle Paul had a powerful transformation in his life when he came in contact with the living Christ. For the rest of his life, He would give Himself fully to make this Jesus known! Paul's passion was for the church of Christ. He wanted them to know and love the Christ that He had come to know and love.

Ephesians chapter one, Paul is writing to a group of people, many of whom He had never met, to encourage them in their new faith. He tells them in verse 15 that since He's heard of their conversion, He hasn't ceased to give thanks for them. Again, we see Paul's heart not being myopic in His thinking. He rejoices anytime someone comes to a saving knowledge of Christ. The kingdom is being crowded, and Paul is rejoicing.

He continues to tell these believers that He's praying for them.

And it is here that we can learn much about Paul's heart for God's people, and how to pray like Paul for the people of God.

He begins by saying that He wants "the eyes of their understanding to be enlightened" (v18). Paul wants believers to see clearly all that God has for them, to know the truth, and to embrace it.

And so, in His prayer, Paul lays out precisely what He's praying for them and what they must clearly see. The first thing is that He wants them to know what "the hope of God's calling for them" is. John Phillips says that this is "the wide sweep of God's eternal purposes in Christ for us." Paul is praying that God's people clearly see the big picture God has ordained for each of them. Ephesians is full of this truth (1:10; 3:10).

Ephesians 2:7-10 tells us that ultimately our eternal purpose is that we are God's "workmanship, created in Christ Jesus for good works." As we are transformed into the image of Christ, our lives shout to the world the exceeding riches of His grace and kindness. That one day, the entire universe—every man, woman, principality, power, and angelic being—will look at those who are standing complete in Jesus Christ, and God will say, "Look what I've done!" This is our ultimate purpose in God's eternal plan, and we must see and know it! The importance of this truth is that, as we let go of this life, we can be assured that no matter what is happening now or where we find ourselves, God has an eternal purpose for us that will not be thwarted—His finished work in our lives and our ultimate glorification.

This truth, when embraced, will help us navigate every storm in our lives, every season, every situation, whether we are facing the mundane, joy, or difficulty in marriage or singleness, raising children, suffering, sickness, dancing, and rejoicing, stress, the unknown, and the known—in all of the mess, joys, and chaos of our lives. Paul wants the eyes of God's people to be open so they can clearly see that they have not been left alone and that they are moving toward the eternal purpose that should give them strength every day and in every circumstance.

"Delight yourself also in the Lord, And He shall give you the desires of your heart."
Psalm 37:4 (NKJV)

But not only do we have an inheritance in Christ, we are an inheritance to Christ. In Ephesians 1:18, it says, "what are the riches of the glory of His inheritance in the saints." The idea is that we get Him, and He gets us, and somehow it is worth it to Him! We are His prize, and we are His joy. Our eyes must be opened to this truth. We are the apple of God's eye; He loves us, and He sings over us. When we understand the love that He has lavished on us, it gives us a sense of value, purpose, and worth that will steady us through this life. The world tries to shape us into its mold and its priorities. Knowing that we are His protects us from being conformed and controlled by this world's empty standards.

The third thing that our eyes must be open to see is "what is the exceeding greatness of the power toward us who believe according to the working of His mighty power, which He worked in Christ when He raised Him from the dead." God's power in creation is unbelievable! But even greater is the power that raised Jesus to life again! This power, the power of the Holy Spirit, now abides in us! We must see clearly that everything that we are commanded to do and be is now possible by the mighty power that is available through the Spirit of God—the same Spirit that raised Christ from the dead. Paul wants believers to know that the most incredible power in the universe resides within them. Everything that we need to live a Spirit-filled life has been given. Now go and do it!

May we pray like Paul for each other and for ourselves! Oh God, open our eyes wide and see these great truths and live them out!!!

In July 2001, Pastor Dressler was called to move his family to Chatham to pastor a church struggling with only 23 people. He, his wife, Kim, and their three sons trusted the Lord and made Canada their new home. They would later add a fourth son, Andy! His plan was simple: preach the Word of God and exalt the Lord Jesus Christ. It has been amazing to watch the Lord bless His work here! Christ has been exalted, and men and women are being drawn to Him. A loving Church and a family atmosphere have blessed us! Our family has grown, too! We have four daughters-in-law and nine grandchildren! We invite you to come and see what God is doing here at Maple City Baptist Church.

"WALKING WITH GOD THROUGH THE PSALMS"

TREVOR BURTON

The moment I was allowed to write an article about the Psalms and prayer, my first thought was to accept it. But a few days after receiving the assignment, I questioned my decision. I was currently going through an uncertain time due to a serious health issue, and I thought to myself, "Am I really prepared to write about the Psalms? How much can I contribute before I even know how it's going to turn out?" The Psalms, also known as the "Book of Prayer" of the Bible, consist of 150 psalms. As you read through the pages of this book, you will read the voices of people from history who lived and worked with God, including kings, shepherds, musicians, and others from communities throughout the world. In their words, you will see the emotions they expressed in their prayer to God.

On November 19, 2025, while driving home from an appointment with my specialist in London, it dawned on me that I had learned a lot, but had not received the answers I anticipated. I was disappointed, but I found some relief by stopping for a Tim Hortons coffee. It was the opportunity to have a peaceful drive home after my appointment that gave me the sense that writing this article was exactly what I needed. The timing was perfect. Instead of dwelling on any disappointments from that day, I was able to reflect on the positive things that had happened in my life. God had heard and answered my prayers.

He had been working and answering my prayers in His time, not mine. God is loving, patient, merciful, and exceedingly faithful to all of us. While I have grown in my prayer life recently, the realization that I have not honestly spent any deliberate time in the Psalms for what feels like far too long hit me hard. It is definitely time to return.

How anyone could condense a writing as incredible as the Psalms into one short article is a nearly impossible task. Many notable authors and theologians have attempted to interpret the rich depth of the Psalms, and even their best efforts barely scratched the surface of the 150 beautiful verses of this priceless book. The Psalms provide the tools necessary to navigate through our fast-paced, chaotic world by helping us to remain focused on our Creator and align ourselves with His purpose for our lives. The Psalms take us through the stages of worship, thanksgiving, lament, confession, and repentance; through each of these experiences of communion with God, we find prayer.

So, what is the purpose of prayer? The purpose of worship is for God to hear us, and because He longs to hear from us. We are His beloved children—so infinitely loved that He sent His only Son, Jesus Christ, to die for us (John 3:16). God desires for us to come to Him with everything, as the Psalms make evident. David, in particular, exemplifies how to express our passionate devotion to God through prayer.

Out of nearly 150 psalms that comprise the book of Psalms, roughly half were written by King David—a man passionately devoted to God who also succumbed to temptation and sin. Psalm 51 is a beautifully heartfelt psalm where David expresses his sorrow for his sin with Bathsheba, while Psalm 23 is arguably the most beloved psalm of all. David has his whole life modeled after his own prayerfulness to God. We see that model lived out through the apostles of the New Testament, particularly Paul, and ultimately through Jesus Christ, who was continually in prayer with the Father and demonstrated for us the perfect prayer in the Lord's Prayer (Matthew 6:9-13).

I have seen firsthand the power of prayer in my life and in the lives of countless others. I cannot begin to describe how beautiful and humbling it is to see someone who may have lost hope or had their expectations shattered when they prayed. I have often been encouraged by others to "pray the Psalms," but to do this, I must know the Psalms. That epiphany reminded me it was time to return to the Psalms.

We all have a favourite psalm; for example, you may have Ps. 91, Ps. 51, Ps. 119 (in its entirety), or Ps. 23.

For myself, in addition to several others, the ones that stand out to me are Psalms 40:1-3 and 34. In Ps. 34:8, King David says, "O taste and see how good the Lord is; blessed is the man who takes refuge in Him." I have tasted and seen that God is good, and I hope everyone reading this has had the same opportunity.

Trevor Burton, a lifelong resident of Chatham-Kent, found salvation at 39 during the COVID pandemic, and began attending Maple City Baptist Church in June 2020, and was baptized at Easter 2021. Growing up in Ridgetown, he always felt like an outsider, never having a sense of belonging to anything. His passion for the arts led him to film school in Toronto, where he graduated with high honors in 2006. But the feeling of being alone never left, which would lead him to face many challenges over the next several years, such as depression and alcoholism, and eventually, he would experience some tragic losses in his late 30s. Once turning to faith in Christ with the guidance of a church friend and mentor, he finally found a place where he belonged and was given a family he could never imagine, a family made up of people just like him, sinners saved by grace. Since then, his focus on film projects has shifted from worldly genres and topics to a faith-based theme, honoring our Lord and Savior Jesus Christ.

1977 JUST A FARMER

The year was 1977, the year we were to be wed. Both of us had finished our university training, graduating with 2 degrees each. Beth was going to start her teaching career in the fall; I was going to take a year off before entering seminary.

During the summers, my brother and I were subcontractors for Blue Water pools, installing above-ground pools. I intended to work from May through the first week of August, before our wedding on August 6. My brother would then finish the installations for the year with a fellow we were training during the season. I would then have to seek employment in September after our honeymoon.

Then came a wrinkle in our plans. A family friend came to us with a golden opportunity. His son worked for a local factory, and he had inside information that they were hiring workers for an afternoon shift.

Having worked for the family before, he said his son would gladly give me a personal recommendation. It would provide me with 16 months of good steady employment that would go a long way in financing my educational pursuits.

Two options were on the table now. Which one should I take? Beth and I wrote out the advantages and the disadvantages of both options. Basically it came down to this.

Would I look to the certainty of a steady income, or would I fulfill my obligations to our family and business? We carefully assessed how each would affect our wedding plans.

The pressure was on. We were approaching a deadline, and a decision had to be made. We asked the Lord for answers, but could not discern any. At times like this, don't you wish you had a direct line to the Lord, where He would pick up the phone and tell you what to do? Then we realized, we do have a way to get specific answers from the Lord. It is in applying the principle of authority that we find in God's Word. 'God reveals His will for our lives through those He has placed in direct authority over us.'

Prov. 21:1, The King's heart is in the hands of the Lord, and as the rivers of water, He turns it wherever He wills. Prov. 11:14 where there is no guidance, the people fail, but in the abundance of counselors, there is victory. So, who was my closest counselor or authority figure? Who was the one who knew me better than anyone else? My Dad. Eph6:1-3. Children obey your parents in the Lord, for this is right. Honor your Father and your Mother [which is the first commandment with a promise] that it may go well with you, and that you may live long on the earth. Eph 6:1-3, Ex.20:12, Deut. 5:16. So, if you really want to know what God's will is, ask those who are directly responsible for you.

The day came. We decided to ask my father. First, Beth and I prayed together, asking God to give us His counsel through my dad.

I fully expected him to tell me to take the factory job. He had gone through difficult times on the farm, and when the opportunity to work regular hours in a business job came, he took it. I assumed the certainty of a paycheck would be the determining factor. His answer surprised me.

He said something like this. "I think you should continue working for the pool company. You and your brother are making good money for now. You are getting married this summer, and you need a honeymoon to start your life as husband and wife. If you took the factory job, you would not have time to get away, and then there is the issue of the afternoon shift. You and Beth would never see each other during the week. You would end up living two separate lives. You need time to bond together as you should. Take the pool job, have a honeymoon, and in the fall, after all the students go back to school, there will be jobs to have."

I was flabbergasted.

He had obviously been thinking about it and was waiting for me to ask. He showed that he had great respect for me as a man, not wanting to interfere in my life, but willing to give counsel when asked. My respect for him as a councilor who cared deeply for our welfare grew considerably. I knew from that time forth, he would be my main sounding board as we navigated the pitfalls of life.

Well, we were married on Aug. 6, 1977. We went on our honeymoon and started our life as husband and wife. September came, and it took me all of 3 days to get a job as a setup mechanic for the local John Deere dealership.

Then came the icing on the cake. About mid-September, our family friend came to us with some breaking news. The factory was laying off all these workers it had hired in the spring and cancelling the afternoon shift. I will never forget what he said next. He said, 'You were wise not to take that job. You would be unemployed now." Perhaps it was wise to seek counsel from those who had life experience. God can use counsel from your parents to direct your life decisions.

PASTOR DAN CHRISTIAANS

Psalm 51 David's Archetypical Prayer of Repentance

David knew how to do many things well. As a shepherd, he fought a bear and a lion. He was a skilled musician who could play instruments and sing heartfelt songs of worship to God. He was a gifted author and songwriter, as demonstrated by his composition of half of the book of Psalms. His bravery in battle is unparalleled as he slew Goliath with a rock and a sling and led men into battle. He is remembered fondly by the Jewish people as Israel's greatest king, and to top it all off, he could dance! David's funeral would have felt like a parade of praises as friends and family gushed over all that he had accomplished for Israel.

However, David was remarkably good at something else: sinning. His rap sheet included adultery, first-degree murder, polygamy, and failing to trust God's power when he ordered a census for his soldiers (resulting in the death of 70,000 Israelites by plague).

To top off the list of his personal sins, his poor parenting led to the rape of his daughter, Tamar, by his son, Amnon, which ended in the murder of Amnon by David's son Absalom. Speaking of Absalom, there was also that time when he attempted to stage a coup against his father, but it ended in Absalom's death in battle.

His sins prevented him from building a temple to honour the Lord as he desired. In modern secular society, politicians can lose their reputations over much more minor mistakes, so why is David still considered Israel's most esteemed king? Even more astonishing is that God refers to David as "A man after my own heart (1 Sam 13:3). The obvious question is, how? How is it possible that David, despite his tendency to sin in significant ways, is still remembered so fondly? The answer lies in one more skill that David had; David was remarkably good at repentance. Psalm 51 serves as a compelling illustration of genuine remorse for one's wrongdoing, recognizing its seriousness, openly admitting it to God, and relying on His grace and mercy. A prayer like this might be what people in today's church need most. Self-righteousness and repentance cannot coexist, and the secret to David's greatness was not his righteousness, but a hatred for his sinfulness. Believers can find several lessons from the model prayer of repentance presented in Psalm 51.

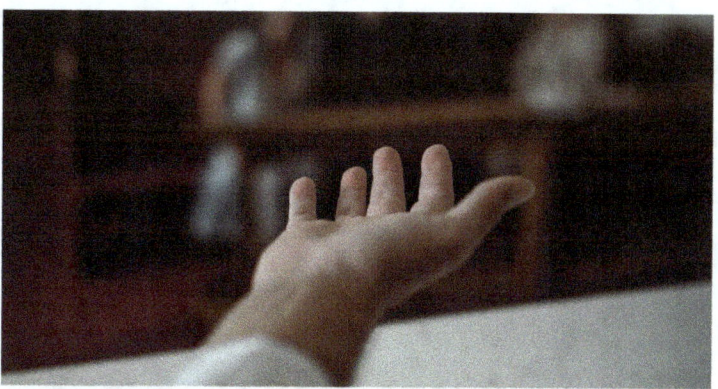

1- **David weighed his sin against the holiness of God, rather than the behaviour of men.** If David had looked at the surrounding nations and the behaviour typical of kings, he would have felt comfortable with his sin. The kings of the earth provided countless examples of behaviour far worse than David's; they would have accepted and even applauded it as his royal entitlement. David did not look to others to define the goodness of his actions. When confronted by Nathan, David realized what he had done. In response, David confessed his sin without any justification. In verse four, he wrote, "Against You, You only, have I sinned, And done this evil in Your sight." This is not to diminish his sin against Bathsheba or Uriah, but rather to recognize that David's sin was first and primarily against God. He refused to love God above all others and instead rebelled against the law God had written on the tablets of Moses and on David's own heart. David is not trying to do damage control or save face; his confession is full of authenticity and contrition because his concern is his relationship with God above anything else.

2-**David did not look inward for answers.** He knew he would not find forgiveness deep within himself, so instead, he confessed his sinful nature and cried out to God. Most believers I know would agree to this statement; however, it is relatively common to see people try to fix their faults with inner reflection and hard work. This can lead to self-justification and either pride or hopelessness, depending on the effort's relative success. The heart of humanity is by nature sinful, and looking inward for the antidote is only going to increase the effectiveness of the poison. David knew there was nothing he could do to contribute to his salvation (v16). Instead, we must be like David who wrote, "I acknowledge my transgressions, and my sin is always before me," and then begged God to, "Wash me thoroughly from my iniquity, and cleanse me from my sin" and again, "Purge me with hyssop, and I shall be clean; wash me, and I shall be whiter than snow", and finally, "Create in me a clean heart, O God, and renew a steadfast spirit within me." David looked to God for the work that only God can do.

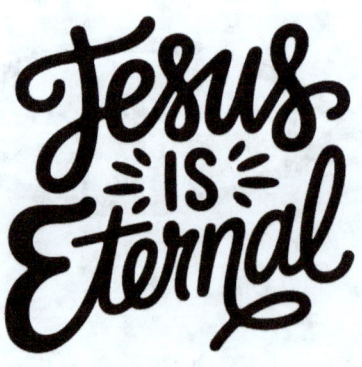

3-**David believed that God could forgive him.** As a pastor, I am not uncommonly hearing fellow believers express an inability to overcome the shame they feel over past sins. Invariably, this shame is rooted in their failure to accept that God really can and does forgive them. When the weight of one's sin finally falls upon an individual (as it must), it can feel crushing. It is a weight that cannot be borne alone; one that is designed to lead the sinner to the Saviour. The enemy will do everything in his power to encourage believers to hold onto the shame, knowing that in doing so, they doubt the power of God and become ineffective witnesses to the grace of God. David came boldly to the throne of grace, believing that God could and would grant him his requests. He believed that, "The sacrifices of God are a broken spirit, a broken and contrite heart - these, O God, You will not despise (v17)." God does not intend believers to live in shame and defeat when He sent His only Son to give them freedom and victory!

4- **David prepared himself to be a trophy of grace.** David believed that God's forgiveness would transform him so thoroughly that he would be a new creature. He looked forward to being cleansed whiter than snow, being filled with joy and gladness, having a clean heart, being in God's presence, and being filled with his Spirit. Though he is facing the wickedness of his heart on full display, David anticipates God's complete forgiveness and his restoration to a right relationship with Him. If that were not enough, he promises that after his restoration, "Then I will teach transgressors Your ways, and sinners shall be converted to You." David is going to tell the world of the goodness of God toward sinners like him. The Apostle Paul echoes this response to God's forgiveness and becomes another trophy of God's grace (1 Tim 1:15-17).

David's prayer of repentance is powerful, in no small part because it was public. David did not try to repent in private for a sin that was publicly known. Instead, he owned up to his mistake and released his prayer of repentance as a song that all of Israel could sing along to. Men like Ezra, Daniel, Nehemiah, and Moses understood the power of public repentance as they went before God on behalf of Israel's sins. Unfortunately, this kind of brutal honesty about sin is rarely found in the church. Believers are not taught that their prayer lives must be drenched in repentance, and as a result, are losing the battle against sin. Sin must be dragged into the light; when a believer confesses his sin, he enlists the power of God to help him overcome and the power of the community to encourage him along. Prayers for comfort, healing, and provision are essential and biblical; however, I believe the prayer in Psalm 51 is most needed by the church of the West today. May we, as the people of God, fall once again at the foot of the cross and confess, knowing that our "God is faithful and just to forgive us of our sin and to cleanse us of all unrighteousness (1Jn 1:8)."

Pastor Dan Christiaans grew up in London, Ontario. At 16, he attended a Christian camp called Camp Y.E.S., where he trusted Christ as his Saviour. God called him to full-time ministry, so he and his wife, Tara, attended FaithWay Bible College of Canada before moving to Chatham to work at Maple City. He has since completed a Bachelor of Science Degree in Religion, a Master's Degree in Pastoral Counseling, and a Doctor of Ministry degree in Expositional Preaching, all through Liberty University. Dan and Tara have served at Maple City for 20 years. In that time, their family has grown significantly; they have been blessed with eight children and continue to serve as foster parents.

Dan loves to serve the church through preaching, teaching and working with the youth and young adults at Maple City.

Discovering the Heart of Communion With God

JEYRAN MAIN

The book of Psalms has long been known as the Bible's prayer book. It is a collection of songs and cries from people who walked closely with God in the highs and lows of life. Through the voices of David, Asaph, Moses, and others, we see what genuine prayer looks like when someone brings their whole heart before the Lord. Every psalm shows us that prayer is not simply a ritual but a relationship with a God who listens, comforts, strengthens, and responds.

We pray because God draws near to those who call on Him. The Psalms remind us again and again that God is attentive to His people: "The LORD is nigh unto all them that call upon him" (Psalm 145:18). Prayer becomes the way we place our fears, joys, burdens, and hopes into His hands. It is how we align our will with His and how we remain connected to His presence in every season of life.

Throughout the Psalms, we find many different kinds of prayer woven together in a beautiful tapestry. Some psalms are filled with praise, lifting God's goodness, power, and faithfulness. Others express thanksgiving, acknowledging His blessings and mercy. Many psalms are written from a place of sorrow or distress, teaching us that God welcomes our tears and struggles.

There are also psalms of confession, such as Psalm 51, in which David pours out his heart and seeks God's cleansing and renewal. And woven through it all are prayers of trust, written by people who chose faith even when they could not yet see God's answers.

One of the most meaningful ways to deepen our prayer life is to pray through the Psalms themselves. When we pray the words of Scripture, we allow God's truth to shape our thoughts, guide our emotions, and anchor our faith. You can begin simply by choosing one psalm and reading it slowly. Let the words settle in your heart. Allow the description of God—whether He is called our refuge, shepherd, shield, or fortress—to become the foundation of your prayer. Speak honestly to Him, just as the psalmists did, and let their words give voice to your own needs and gratitude. Even when a psalm begins in pain or confusion, it nearly always ends in trust, reminding us to place our hope in God regardless of our circumstances.

The Psalms teach us that prayer is a journey. It weaves through moments of joy and moments of heaviness, through confession and praise, through pleading and thanksgiving.

Prayer is not about perfect wording but about a sincere heart that seeks God.

The psalmists show us that we can be honest, vulnerable, and confident when we come before the Lord, knowing that He hears every whisper.

As you explore this beautiful book, may it draw you closer to God and deepen your understanding of prayer. If you have never prayed through the Psalms before, consider beginning with Psalm 1 and continuing from there. Let each chapter guide you, comfort you, and lead you into a richer communion with your Heavenly Father.

The Psalms remind us that our prayers matter. They rise to the One who loves us, listens to us, and walks with us every step of the way.

Jeyran Main has spent years immersed in the world of books as an editor and publisher. She is the author of The Radical Realism of Jesus: A Framework for Living in the 21st Century and God's Surprising Ways: The Path to Lasting Joy, Healing, and Love. Through her platform, HeavenlyHarmonyHub.com, she offers resources that inspire thoughtful engagement with faith. Guided by a passion for truth, she explores how God's counterintuitive Kingdom wisdom overturns human expectations and invites readers into a life of joy, healing, generosity, and love.

THE OLD TESTAMENT: TO READ OR TO REJECT?

ETHAN DAVENPORT

Why should we read the Old Testament? I mean, it's called the "Old Testament" for a reason, right? In recent times, well-known Christian leaders have argued that we ought to "unhitch" ourselves from the first part of our Bible. "Peter, James, and Paul elected to unhitch the Christian faith from their Jewish scriptures, and my friends, we must as well," one pastor says.

While most of us recognize the danger posed by such a statement, I'm afraid many born-again believers operate this way. When was the last time you seriously read through Ezekiel, aiming at comprehension and understanding its context? Can you describe the historical backdrop of Amos's writing? What is the overall storyline of the Old Testament? Questions like these—and our inability to answer them—demonstrate our neglect toward almost three-quarters of the Bible!

This temptation, however novel it may seem to us, is actually almost as old as Christianity itself. Around AD 140, a Sinopean man named Marcion began to adopt the beliefs of the Gnostic teacher Cerdo. Cerdo, originally a follower of Simon Magus (Simon the Magician), taught that the Old Testament God was different from the God of the New Testament.

The former was an evil god of justice, and the latter was merciful and gracious. Marcion took this teaching and ran with it. The Old Testament God, Marcion said, was the author of evil and concerned only for the people of Israel. The New Testament God, on the other hand, was full of love and compassion for all people. Because of this, Marcion rejected the entire Old Testament, as well as any New Testament documents that he thought favoured Jewish readers.

By the time Marcion had turned off his metaphorical shredder, he was left with only a portion of the Gospel of Luke and ten of the Pauline epistles. Paul, judged Marcion, was the only apostle who did not corrupt the gospel of Christ. Marcion's teaching spread like wildfire. Marcionite churches, appearing like orthodox congregations, started popping up left and right. Even as late as the fourth century, the Sinopean Gnostics' teaching still prospered in villages near Damascus.

In the face of this problem, the Orthodox Church found herself at a crossroads. Should she accept Marcion's dismissal of the Hebrew Tanakh, or dismiss the writings of Paul that the Marcionites pointed to in defence of their claims? In God's providence, the Church chose neither option. Instead, the Church retained the Old Testament while also pointing out that Paul himself saw in Christ not only perfect grace but also perfect justice. As historian Bruce Shelley notes, "Paul found in the cross not only a demonstration of God's love but also a display of his righteousness. Christ's death, he said, allowed God to be both just and the justifier of all who believe in Jesus (Rom. 3:25–26). That is the marvel of the grace of God that Marcion missed."[1] Marcion was condemned as a heretic and an antichrist, being excommunicated from the Church in Rome around AD 144.

Why was Marcion wrong? After all, the Church is the people of the new covenant, not the old (Jer. 31:31–37). The author of Hebrews writes, "In speaking of a new covenant, he makes the first one obsolete. And what is becoming obsolete and growing old is ready to vanish away" (Heb. 8:13). The problem with Marcionite teaching is that it denies what Scripture plainly teaches. First, it denies what Paul asserts: that "All Scripture"—even the Old Testament—"is profitable for teaching, for reproof, for correction, and for training in righteousness" (2 Tim. 3:16). Second, it denies the biblical-theological framework through which the apostles viewed the events of the New Testament. Stephen Wellum explains this truth skillfully: "Jesus Christ does not appear de novo in the New Testament, that is, out of thin air. Instead, who Jesus is and what he has done in his redemptive work is entirely dependent on the…content and structures of the Old Testament. Unless we ground the gospel first in the Old Testament, we will quickly lose the central truths of Christian theology." Wellum goes on to remark, "given our lack of knowing the Old Testament, it is not surprising that the theological life and health of today's evangelical church is in trouble."[2] He's right.

The New Testament is clear that new covenant believers are not "under the law" as a covenant (Gal. 5:18). Nevertheless, the Hebrew Bible continues to serve as Scripture for us.

The Old Testament, as God-breathed, demands our complete devotion, study, and obedience. While the law-covenant of Moses is not binding on new-covenant believers, the Bible must be read covenantally. Ditching or "unhitching" the Christian faith from the Old Testament is disastrous precisely because it is the very foundation on which the apostolic message stands.

---

1 Bruce Shelley, Church History in Plain Language (Grand Rapids: Zondervan Academic, 2008), 77.
2 Stephen J. Wellum, "Foreword," in Delighting in the Old Testament: Through Christ and for Christ, by Jason DeRouchie (Wheaton, IL: Crossway, 2024), xv–xvi.

The New Testament makes sense only in light of the Old Testament, and the Old Testament finds its whole meaning only in light of the New Testament. Jesus is the better Adam and the better Moses (Rom. 5:14; Heb. 3:1–6). He is the fulfillment of God's covenant oath to Abraham and David (Gen. 12:2–3; 2 Sam. 7:9–16; Gal. 3:16, 29). He is the one whom God promised would crush Satan's head and remove the curse of sin (Gen. 3:15). The Old Testament points to its fulfillment in Christ's atoning work. Without the Old Testament, the New Testament makes no sense.

When we approach the Bible this way—looking to the apostles to teach us how to read the Old Testament—instead of merely skimming over the words during our morning devotions while the coffee brews, we are amazed! We discover a glorious unity in the Bible's storyline. On the road to Emmaus, the resurrected Christ encountered two men.

Failing to recognize him, the men spoke about "Jesus of Nazareth, a man who was a prophet mighty in deed and word before God and all the people, and how our chief priests and rulers delivered him up to be condemned to death, and crucified him. But we had hoped he was the one to redeem Israel." Jesus, far from commending their sympathy toward him, rebukes the men: "'O foolish ones, and slow of heart to believe all that the prophets have spoken! Was it not necessary that the Christ should suffer these things and enter into his glory?' And beginning with Moses and all the Prophets, he interpreted to them in all the Scriptures the things concerning himself." Later, when Jesus was having dinner with the men, "he took the bread and blessed and broke it and gave it to them." At this moment, the men must have seen the scars on Jesus's wrists. "Their eyes were opened, and they recognized him. ... They said to each other, 'Did not our hearts burn within us while he talked to us on the road, while he opened to us the Scriptures?'" (Luke 24:13–32). On the road, the men, like many God-fearing Jews, still misunderstood their Messiah's mission. What did Jesus do to combat this? He opened the Old Testament. Read your Bible.

SCRIPTURES SCHOOL OF PRAYER

PASTOR ANDREW MCCOMBE

Prayer is a curious thing. It is most unnatural for a human being to humbly acknowledge anything outside of themself. Yet, prayer is to humbly admit that something is lacking within, something insufficient that requires an outside answer. Prayer connects the creature with the creator. The Bible tells us that this degree of connection is only made possible by the blood of God's Son, Jesus Christ. Through Christ's work on the cross, the sinful nature of man is dealt with, giving man an opportunity to repent of his sin and place his faith solely on the finished work of Jesus Christ. Herein lies the dichotomy. To those who are perishing, prayer is foolishness, but to those who are being saved, it is a means of communing with the God of Heaven and Earth. While this article will not be able to present an exhaustive work of scriptures' treatment of prayer, it will endeavor to highlight three things that scripture prescribes in regards to prayer.

Pray Without Ceasing

First, Scripture teaches the believer that they are to pray without ceasing. While the believer should stop and take time each day to pray, Paul tells us in 1 Thessalonians 5:17 that the believer is never to leave a state of prayerfulness. While a believer is still called to fulfill their daily duty, the believer in Christ should never escape a sense of consciousness that they are in the presence of the Lord. They should consistently bring things before the Lord in prayer, and they should view everything they encounter through the lens of this fellowship with their heavenly Father.

Pray Expectantly

In 1 John 5;14 we read; Now this is the confidence that we have in Him, that if we ask anything according to His will, He hears us. A born-again believer can begin the day with the confidence that not only does God hear their prayer, but He answers it. In Psalm 5:3, the Psalmist proclaims that he arises early in the day to pray, and then waits expectantly as the day goes on to see his prayer answered. We should imitate the boldness and the confidence of the Psalmist in praying expectantly. We are no longer at enmity with God; Christ's work is complete, and therefore, we can, and we must, approach the throne of grace in boldness and in confidence.

Pray according to God's Will

Finally, when we pray, we are to pray according to God's will. If we return to 1 John 5:14, John instructs us how we are to come before the Lord in prayer; we are to pray according to His will. In humility, as we come to the Lord, we are reminded that it is not our kingdom we are building, but God's. To know God's will is to know what God has revealed about Himself through His Word. Simply, Christians are to know the Word of God and to pray the Word of God.

By praying without ceasing, praying expectantly, and praying according to God's will, the believer can look forward to a warm and robust life of prayer as they seek to glorify God and enjoy Him forever.

Andrew McCombe, originally from London, Ontario, earned his teaching degree at Liberty University, where he met his wife, Stacey. After teaching at Chatham Christian School for eight years, Andrew felt called to full-time ministry at MCBC. He is currently pursuing his Master of Divinity and has spent the last eight years serving in various ministries at MCBC. Andrew is dedicated to encouraging families to stand for truth and values growing a strong foundation in faith. He and Stacey, who have four children, cherish their time serving the MCBC community.

www.ingramcontent.com/pod-product-compliance
Lightning Source LLC
Chambersburg PA
CBHW051432070526

44584CB00023B/3689